D1483253

Slugs, Snails, and Worms

Trudi Strain Trueit

Cavendish
Square

New York

Published in 2014 by Cavendish Square Publishing, LLC
303 Park Avenue South, Suite 1247, New York, NY 10010

Copyright © 2014 by Cavendish Square Publishing, LLC

First Edition

Library of Congress Cataloging-in-Publication Data

Trueit, Trudi Strain.
Slugs, snails, and worms / Trudi Strain Trueit.
p. cm. — (Backyard safari)
Summary: "Identify specific slugs, snails, and worms. Explore their behavior,
life cycle, mating habits, geographical location, anatomy, enemies, and defenses"—Provided by publisher.
Includes bibliographical references and index.
ISBN 978-1-60870-247-3 (hardcover) • ISBN 978-1-62712-030-2 (paperback) • ISBN 978-1-60870-820-8 (ebook)
1. Slugs (Mollusks)—Juvenile literature. 2. Snails—Juvenile literature. 3. Worms—Juvenile literature. I. Title.
QL430.4T88 2013
594'.3—dc23
2011026619

Editor: Christine Florie
Art Director: Anahid Hamparian
Series Designer: Alicia Mikles

Expert Reader: Diarmaid Ó Foighil, Professor of Ecology and Evolutionary Biology, Director, Museum of Zoology, University of Michigan, Ann Arbor

Photo research by Marybeth Kavanagh

Cover photo by age fotostock/SuperStock
The photographs in this book are used by permission and through the courtesy of: *Alamy*: blickwinkel, 4; Premaphotos, 15; imagebroker, 18; Neil Hardwick, 22LL; WILDLIFE GmbH, 22LR, 23LL; Florida Images, 23LR; Nigel Cattlin, 24R; *Getty Images*: George Grall/National Geographic, 5; *SuperStock*: age fotostock, 6, 17, 26; imagebroker.net, 8; Animals Animals, 9, 10, 21, 24L; Mauritius, 23TR; *Dorling Kindersley*: 11; Howard Shooter, 14TL; *Media Bakery*: Veer, 14ML, 14MR; *Cutcaster*: Miro Kovacevic, 14TR; Sergej Razvodovskij, 14 (bottom); *Minden Pictures*: Gerry Ellis, 16; *The Image Works*: Roehrbein/ullstein bild, 22TL; The Natural History Museum, 23TL; *Ardea*: Duncan Usher, 22TR; *Corbis*: Ed Murray/Star Ledger, 25; Gary Braasch, 27

Printed in the United States of America

Contents

Introduction

Have you ever watched baby spiders hatch from a silky egg sac? Or seen a butterfly sip nectar from a flower? If you have, you know how wonderful it is to discover nature for yourself. Each book in the Backyard Safari series takes you step-by-step on an easy outdoor adventure, then helps you identify the animals you've found. You'll also learn ways to attract, observe, and protect these valuable creatures. As you read, be on the lookout for the Safari Tips and Trek Talk facts sprinkled throughout the book. Ready? The fun starts just steps from your back door!

ONE

In No Hurry

Do you stay inside on rainy days? You might change your mind if you knew how much was happening outside. Snails are munching on plants. Earthworms are wiggling through the grass. Slugs are leaving gooey trails across the sidewalk. It's a soggy world of activity!

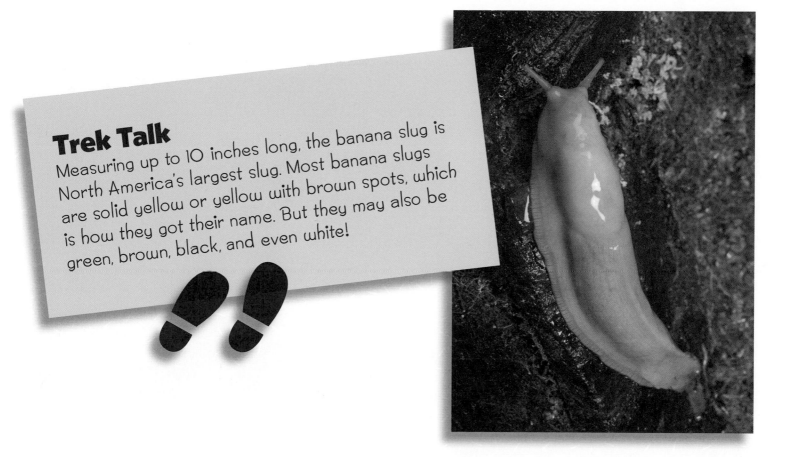

Trek Talk
Measuring up to 10 inches long, the banana slug is North America's largest slug. Most banana slugs are solid yellow or yellow with brown spots, which is how they got their name. But they may also be green, brown, black, and even white!

Watch Your Step

Slugs and snails are part of one of the largest groups of animals on the planet, the **mollusks**. Mollusks have soft bodies with no backbones. Some also have shells. Oysters, clams, and octopuses are mollusks, too. Many kinds of slugs and snails live in ponds, lakes, and oceans, while others live on land.

Slugs and snails are **gastropods**, a word that means "stomach foot." A gastropod's body is called a foot. Strong muscles within the foot push and pull in waves to move the creature along. Slugs also have a skirt, a ridge that runs around the bottom edge of the foot. Sometimes the skirt is the same color as a slug's body. Other times it may stand out, like the bright red or orange fringe of the European red slug. Slugs and snails that live on land have several glands that are constantly releasing **mucus**. This slime has many purposes. It helps the animal stay moist, move, mark a trail, find a mate,

European red slugs are common in the Pacific Northwest. They are recognized by their red or orange fringe.

Slime Machines

Gastropods use their mucus to safely slide across almost any surface— even broken glass. When the animal stops, the goo hardens and anchors the foot. It sticks so well that a gastropod can cling upside down without falling. Such remarkable abilities led engineers at the Massachusetts Institute of Technology to build a robot that can glide along human-made slime. They say that in the future robotic slugs could be used for all kinds of things, including going inside the human body to help treat disease.

and reach food. Mucus is vital for protection, too. **Predators**, such as frogs, snakes, and birds, will often stay away from a slug covered in slick, distasteful mucus.

A gastropod has a fleshy lobe on its back called a **mantle**. The mantle forms a lung sac for breathing. In snails the mantle also produces calcium to make a shell. While a slug uses its mucus for protection, a snail relies on its shell for self-defense. Snail shells grow in a spiral pattern. Each circle in the spiral is called a whorl. The shape of its shell is different for every type of snail. Some of the most common shapes look like cones, eggs, spires, or cinnamon rolls. A slug does not have an outer shell. Many types of slugs, however, have an inner shell located under the skin of their mantles. Scientists say this platelike shell is likely the remnant of what was once an outer shell millions of years ago.

Snails are mollusks. They have soft bodies and hard shells.

A gastropod's head typically has two pairs of **tentacles** and a mouth. The upper tentacles have tiny, light-sensitive eyes. The lower tentacles are used for feeling and tasting. Inside the mouth is a **radula**, a ribbon-like tongue with more than 25,000 tiny teeth. Slugs and snails spend much of their time eating. Many eat their own weight in food every single day! They feed mainly on fungi and the leaves and roots of plants. A few **prey** on each other.

Slugs and snails have both male and female sex organs. A gastropod may lay and fertilize its own eggs, but only if it cannot find a mate. It lays up to a hundred little round eggs in the dirt or under leaves. The eggs take three to twelve weeks to hatch, depending on the type of slug. The hatchlings will grow to be adults in a few months. Backyard gastropods typically live from one to six years.

Slugs lay small masses of eggs. The eggs hatch within three to twelve weeks.

A Wiggler's World

Dig a few inches into rich, moist soil and you'll probably find an earthworm. These squirming critters belong to a group of segmented worms called Oligochaete (AWL-i-go-keet), meaning "few hairs." Earthworms have tiny hairs, or bristles, on their bodies called **setae** (see-tee). When a worm wants to move, it grips the soil with its back setae and squeezes its circular muscles (this lengthens its body). Some of the front setae then grip the soil and the back setae let go. The worm squeezes its lengthwise muscles (making its body shorter) and the back sections can now move forward. Setae also come in handy when a frog, bird, or other predator tries to yank the worm out of the soil. The worm digs in and holds on. Some worms may regrow a head or tail if it's lost to

Earthworms use the motion of their muscles and their setae to burrow into soil.

a predator, but only if the injury isn't too severe. Like gastropods, earthworms also release mucus. The slime keeps the worm moist, helps with mating, and aids in self-defense. When threatened, an earthworm may shoot a tiny stream of mucus at its attacker.

An earthworm has no eyes, ears, or nose, but it does have a mouth (without teeth). As a worm moves through the soil, it eats soil filled with decaying roots, leaves, dead animal matter, and other nutrients.

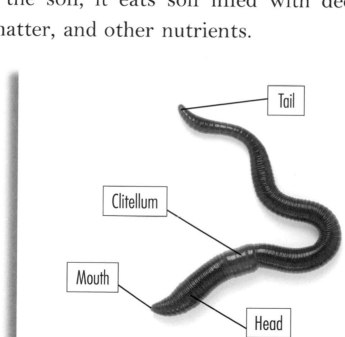

Tail

Clitellum

Mouth

Head

Earthworms have ringlike segments covering their bodies. An earthworm's mouth is found at the first segment.

Like gastropods, earthworms have male and female sex organs. Unlike slugs and snails, they always need a partner to reproduce. After transferring sperm packets with a mate, an earthworm produces mucus from its **clitellum** (kly-TELL-um) to form an egg sac, or cocoon, around its body. The clitellum is a longer, thicker segment that is either lighter, darker, or a different color from the other segments. Once the cocoon forms, the earthworm slides backward. This allows the eggs and sperm to slip into the egg sac. The cocoon then slides off the head and is sealed. A few weeks later baby earthworms emerge from the cocoon. Earthworms can live from one to eight years.

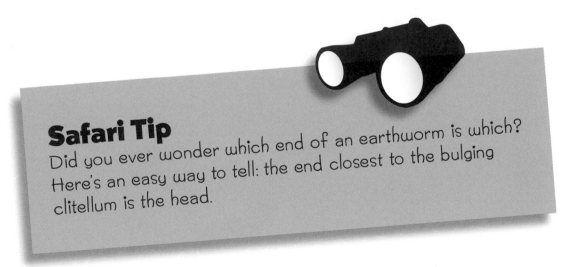

Safari Tip
Did you ever wonder which end of an earthworm is which? Here's an easy way to tell: the end closest to the bulging clitellum is the head.

Knowing more about the slugs, snails, and worms will help you enjoy your safari. Are you ready for your adventure? Let's go!

TWO
You Are the Explorer

Gastropods and earthworms thrive in cool, dark, damp areas. You'll want to search for them during rainy seasons. Choose a cloudy, calm day when the temperature is between 50° and 65° Fahrenheit. Try to go out after a good rainstorm. Slugs, snails, and worms are most active at night, but these soil-dwellers will be out in the morning if the ground is wet. When going on safari, it's wise to leave all pets at home.

Trek Talk
During a hot summer or cold winter a snail may seal itself inside its shell with mucus and calcium to wait for milder, wetter weather. Some desert snails have been known to remain alive sealed inside their shells for several years!

What Do I Wear?

* A rain hat
* A long-sleeved, waterproof jacket
* Jeans or other long pants
* Waterproof boots

What Do I Take?

* Magnifying glass
* Digital camera
* Garden trowel for digging
* Plastic ruler
* Notebook
* Colored pens or pencils
* A few sheets of paper towels
* Umbrella

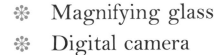

Where Do I Go?

Slugs, snails, and earthworms will be attracted to these things in your backyard:

* ❋ A flower bed or vegetable garden
* ❋ Tall grasses
* ❋ Piles of autumn leaves
* ❋ **Compost** or mulch piles
* ❋ Under dead trees, stumps, or logs
* ❋ Stacked firewood, bottom pieces
* ❋ Beneath loose stepping stones or patio bricks

Garden snails and slugs feed on a compost heap.

If you don't have a backyard or your backyard doesn't offer any of these features, try these locations:

* Meadows
* Woodlands
* Fields
* Garden nurseries
* Public parks

Always have an adult with you if you are going beyond your backyard. Be sure to stay on public property.

Trek Talk
Many slugs and snails will climb trees to eat fresh leaves. Some, like the milky slug, will hang upside down, held only by a thick string of mucus, to reach their favorite leaves.

What Do I Do?

✳ Begin your safari by looking for holes in the leaves of low-growing plants. These are clues that gastropods have been dining while you were sleeping. Use your magnifying glass to search through the leaves, stems, and soil for slugs and snails. Do you see a trail of shiny slime? Follow it!

Use a magnifying glass to look for slime trails and holes in leaves.

Safari Tip

While turning over leaves in your hunt for gastropods, you may get some of their slime on your hands. Resist the temptation to wash it off right then. Mucus is designed to absorb water, so running your hands under the faucet will only create more of a mess. Instead, wipe your hands well with a paper towel. Once the slime is gone, *then* wash with soap and water. A little white vinegar may also help clean off any stubborn slime.

* Look for gastropods and earthworms in piles of leaves, compost, and mulch. Remember to check under loose patio stones or bricks, around logs and stumps, and in stacks of firewood.

* If you have a flower or vegetable garden, search for gastropods on the leaves and stems of lilies, primroses, begonias, hostas, strawberries, and lettuce. To find earthworms, use your trowel to gently dig 5 or 6 inches into moist soil. Be careful that you don't accidentally cut up any worms!

* When you find a slug, snail, or earthworm, make an entry in your notebook. What are its main colors? For slugs and snails, does it have spots, blotches, or other **field marks**? What color are its tentacles and skirt? Is its skin smooth or rough? Describe the colors, patterns, and shape of a snail's shell. For earthworms, what color is the clitellum? Use your ruler to measure the animal's length. Note where you found it and what it was doing. Leave a blank line on the bottom of your entry to add its name later.

Be sure to write your findings in a notebook.

※ Take a photograph or use your colored pencils to make a sketch of your discovery.

SLUG

Colors: tan foot, tan skirt, dark-brown tentacles

Field Marks: leopard-like spots on mantle and foot

Skin: smooth

Size: 4 inches long

Location/Activity: on leaf, eating

Name: _____

Your Drawing or Photo Goes Here

※ Spend about a half hour to an hour on safari.
※ Clean up the area and take everything with you when you leave.

Did you like searching for slugs, snails, and worms? Don't be discouraged if you didn't come across many slippery creatures. Wait for another rainstorm and try again! When you are back inside, download and print any photos you took. It's time now to learn more about your discoveries!

THREE
A Guide to Slugs, Snails, and Worms

Your safari may be over, but there is more fun ahead in identifying the animals you have uncovered. First, gather your notebook and photos. Paste each photo next to its entry. Starting with your first animal, flip through the pages in this chapter to find its category. Below are some questions you'll want to ask yourself as you compare your animals to those in the field guide.

* **Slug**: What is its main color? Does it have spots, blotches, or other field marks? Is its skin smooth or rough? What colors are the tentacles and skirt? How big is the slug?
* **Snail**: What is its body color? What is the shape of the shell? What colors and patterns make up the shell? How many whorls do you count? How big is the snail?
* **Earthworm**: What color is it? What color is the clitellum? How long is the worm?

If you spot your discovery in the field guide, good work! Write the animal's name in the space you left for it in your notebook.

SLUG

Colors: tan foot, tan skirt, brown tentacles

Field Marks: leopard-like spots on mantle and foot

Skin: smooth

Size: 4 inches long

Location/Activity: on leaf, eating

Name: great gray garden slug

If you find you're having trouble making a match, don't worry. North America has, at least, forty types of slugs, two hundred kinds of earthworms, and seven hundred different snails—far too many to feature here. Also, many of the same gastropods come in various colors, which can make identifying them tricky. Worms, on the other hand, can look so much alike it can be hard to tell one type from another. Use the resources in the Find Out More section in the back of this book for additional help with identifying your specimens.

Slug Guide

European Black Slug

European Red Slug

Tree Slug

Field Slug

Snail Guide

Brown Garden Snail

Brown-lipped Snail

White-lipped Snail

Florida Tree Snail

Worm Guide

Night Crawler

Tiger Worm

FOUR
Try This!
Projects You Can Do

Slugs, snails, and earthworms may be small, but they play a big role on Earth. Day and night, these expert eaters are breaking down plant and animal matter into compost, adding nutrients to our soil. As these animals move, they mix the compost with oxygen, water, and other nutrients. This makes the soil healthier—and healthy soil means stronger roots for grasses, vegetables, flowers, and trees. Also, gastropods help scatter seeds so that new plants may grow. Try the following projects to learn more about why these soil-dwellers are so valuable to our planet.

Trek Talk
An acre of good quality soil may be home to more than a million earthworms, including night crawlers. On cool, wet evenings, night crawlers will come to the surface to eat decaying leaves and dead insects. These large worms are among the best diggers of the earthworm family, tunneling as far as 7 feet underground!

Gastropod Ramp

Do you want to see for yourself the wavelike way gastropods move? You'll need a sheet of heavy, clear plastic, about 10 or 11 inches long, to use as a ramp. Find a flat spot in the garden area you are testing. Prop up one end of the plastic ramp with stones so that it sits at an angle about 5 inches off the ground. Place a strawberry or piece of lettuce at the top of the ramp to encourage a gastropod to head up it (it's okay to place the animal at the bottom of the ramp; just be *very* gentle). As it slowly travels up the ramp, lie on the ground to watch the motion of its foot from underneath the clear plastic. Snap a few photos and make some notes in your notebook. When you have finished observing the gastropod (and it's done eating), carefully place the tiny animal back where you found it.

Snail Shelter

Give snails a cool, wet, dark place to call home. Find an old clay flowerpot. Using a garden hose, soak the pot with water. Place the pot upside down in a garden near flowers or vegetables. Prop up one side of the pot with a sturdy

Clay flowerpots can be used to create shelters for snails.

rock so snails can get inside. That's it! Check the shelter every few days to see if you have any gastropod guests. During the summer gently wet down the clay pot every day or two to keep it moist.

Aloha, Snails

Found only in Hawaii, Oahu tree snails were once so plentiful their colorful cone-shaped shells were used in leis and ornaments. But today these snails, barely bigger than your pinky nail, are on the brink of **extinction**. Thirty of the forty-one types of Oahu tree snails can no longer be found. The U.S. Fish and Wildlife Service says the main threats to these animals are habitat destruction and predators, such as rats and larger snails. Oahu tree snails are now protected by law. Officials are also considering setting up snail colonies to keep these tiny national treasures from disappearing forever.

Compost Pod

Recycle your kitchen leftovers, while inviting earthworms to do their stuff. In early spring choose an area in your yard where you will eventually want to plant a flower. Dig a hole about 1 foot wide and 2 feet deep. Get some adult help for this if you need to. Place three cups of fruit and vegetable scraps, such as banana peels, lettuce leaves, and/or orange rinds, into the hole. Add a thin layer of dead leaves or pine needles. Fill the hole with soil. Wait a few months for bugs and earthworms to break down the matter into compost. By early summer, your compost pod will be ready to feed the roots of a flower. Plant your flower in the middle of the compost pod and watch what happens!

A sky packed with gray rain clouds may not be a welcome sight to many humans. But now you know just how important water is to the small, slow, slippery animals that make their homes not far from yours. You also know how easy it is to find slugs, snails, and worms any time you want. Are those raindrops on the roof? Grab your umbrella and let's go!

Glossary

clitellum   the thickest segment of an earthworm, which releases mucus to form an egg sac

compost   decaying plant and animal matter that adds nutrients to the soil

extinction   the dying out of a type of animal or plant

field marks   spots, blotches, or other distinguishing marks on an animal

gastropods   a subgroup of mollusks that includes slugs and snails

mantle   the thick, fleshy lobe on the back of a gastropod that forms a lung sac and, in snails, produces calcium for a shell

mollusks   a group of animals characterized by a soft body and no backbone and that may have a shell

mucus   a slimy mixture of fluids secreted by the body

predators   animals that hunt other animals for food

prey   to grab and eat

radula   a flexible tonguelike organ with rows of tiny, sharp teeth

setae   stiff hairs or bristles

tentacles   thin feelers an animal uses for taste, touch, and smell

Find Out More

Books

Lunis, Natalie. *Wiggly Earthworms*. New York: Bearport Publishing, 2009.

Rustad, Martha E. H. *Snails*. Mankato, MN: Capstone Press, 2010.

Silverstein, Alvin, Virginia B. Silverstein, and Laura Silverstein Nunn. *Dung Beetles, Slugs, Leeches, and More: The Yucky Animal Book*. Berkeley Heights, NJ: Enslow, 2010.

DVDs

Snails: Backyard Science, Phoenix Learning Group, 2008.

Worm Bin Creatures Alive Through a Microscope, Flowerfield Enterprises/Warren Hatch, 2009.

Websites

The Adventures of Herman the Worm

http://urbanext.illinois.edu/worms

Log on to this kid-friendly website to explore the history and life of an earthworm. It includes easy-to-read anatomy information, fun facts, and links to other worm sites.

BioKIDS: Gastropods

www.biokids.umich.edu/critters/Gastropoda/

Learn more about how gastropods grow, eat, and reproduce. You'll also find photos of common North American slugs and snails at this educational website.

National Geographic: Invertebrates

http://animals.nationalgeographic.com/animals/invertebrates.html

Log on to this website to see stunning photographs and fascinating facts about earthworms and mollusks.

Index

Page numbers in **boldface** are illustrations.

About the Author

TRUDI STRAIN TRUEIT specializes in writing about nature and weather. She is the author of more than eighty fiction and nonfiction books for children, including *Ants, Grasshoppers,* and *Dragonflies* in the Backyard Safari series. The author was born and raised in the soggy Pacific Northwest—home to all things slimy, including the banana slug (one once left a slick trail across her sleeping bag at camp!). She has a B.A. degree in broadcast journalism. Trueit lives in Everett, Washington, with her husband, Bill, a high school photography teacher, and their three cats. Visit her website at www.truditrueit.com.